SAMMY
the Sand Dollar

Written & Illustrated by:

 Nina Leipold

Palmetto Publishing Group, LLC
www.PalmettoPublishingGroup.com

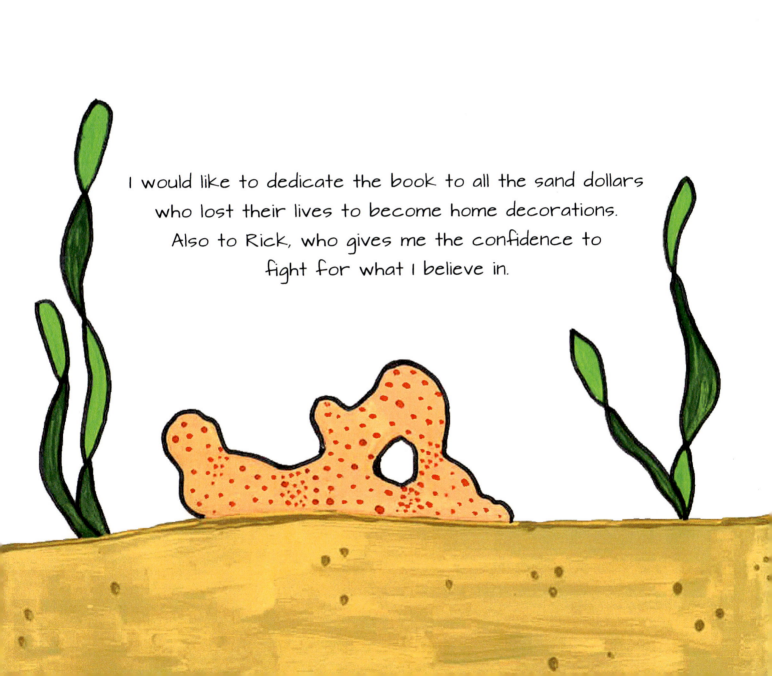

I would like to dedicate the book to all the sand dollars
who lost their lives to become home decorations.
Also to Rick, who gives me the confidence to
fight for what I believe in.

Sammy the sand dollar lives on the bottom of the ocean, where he likes to dig in the sand and play with his friends, Lily the dolphin and Stu the starfish. They explore the ocean and nearby saltwater creeks and rivers.

1

Sammy, Lily, and Stu like to swim, play, and explore all day long. There is nothing they enjoy more than making new friends and discovering new, exciting things. They go on many adventures together.

One day, Sammy, Lily, and Stu are exploring in the ocean when they see a nearby beach where people are playing. They want to learn more about people, so they swim closer to shore.

Lily and Stu are playing when they realize Sammy is no longer with them. He has somehow become separated from their group. Lily and Stu search everywhere.

"Sammy!" they yell, but there is no answer.

7

Sammy can't hear his friends because he's too busy having fun. Sammy is caught up in his own adventure. He's digging and playing in the sand, very close to where the people are playing.

Suddenly, a hand comes down into the water, digs Sammy out of the sand, and picks him up.

"I see him!" says Lily. "He's in trouble!"

Lily and Stu know that if Sammy is out of the water too long, he won't be able to live and will turn into a white skeleton, which is called a test. There is nothing Lily and Stu can do to stop this from happening, and this worries them.

Out of nowhere, a boy screams, "Stop! Stop, Mom!"

It's Ricky the kid. His mother is the person who took Sammy from his ocean home. Ricky is Sammy's only chance to be saved, and he knows it!

"What's wrong, Ricky?" his mother asks.

Ricky replies, "Mom, that sand dollar is alive. Don't you see? If you take him out of the ocean, he'll die!"

Ricky's mother says, "Don't be silly, Ricky. This sand dollar is not moving, so it is not alive. How can something that doesn't move be alive? Also, it will be a good decoration in our house."

Ricky looks at Sammy, who is already struggling to breathe, then looks out into the ocean and sees Lily and Stu crying over their friend. Ricky knows his mother is wrong. Ricky knows that Sammy is a living thing.

"Mom, look at him! He has a home and friends just like me!" Ricky says.

His mother looks into the ocean and notices Lily and Stu waiting for their friend to be returned to them. Ricky's mother realizes that what her son told her is true.

"You're right, Ricky," she says. "Just because I don't see him moving doesn't mean he isn't alive. He has friends and a home, just like you said."

Then, Ricky's mom gently places Sammy back in the ocean.

Relieved and excited to be alive, Sammy hurries back to his worried friends, who are happy to see him and begin celebrating his return.

Lily and Stu embrace Sammy in a big hug but soon realize they shouldn't stay in shallow water much longer because there are other people who might find them. They all swim back into the deeper ocean, where they're safe from people. But before their return, Sammy looks back and waves to Ricky.

"Thank you!" Sammy yells out to Ricky. "You saved my life! I'll never forget you!"

Ricky the kid just smiles because he knew all along that Sammy was alive, and he is glad that he could be a hero today.

27

About the Author

Nina Leipold, originally from Pennsylvania, now lives on Hilton Head Island in South Carolina. Aquatic conservation is extremely important to her; she's a former dolphin trainer, and she worked with the real Lily the dolphin (pictured). She is a certified SCUBA diver, and is working toward her captain's license.

Leipold was inspired to write her first children's book, *Sammy the Sand Dollar*, after seeing so many people unknowingly kill sand dollars by removing them from the ocean for home decorating purposes. Through her writing, Leipold hopes to educate children on the importance of nature conservation.

Made in the USA
San Bernardino, CA
11 August 2016